EDGE BOOKS™

WILD ABOUT SNAKES

KINGSNAKES

BY HEATHER L. MONTGOMERY

Consultant:

Edge Books are published by Capstone Press,
151 Good Counsel Drive, P.O. Box 669, Mankato, Minnesota 56002.
www.capstonepub.com

 Books published by Capstone Press are manufactured with paper
containing at least 10 percent post-consumer waste.

Library of Congress Cataloging-in-Publication Data
Montgomery, Heather L.
  Kingsnakes / by Heather L. Montgomery.
     p. cm.—(Wild about snakes)
  Includes index.
  ISBN 978-1-4296-6013-6 (library binding)
  ISBN 978-1-4296-7285-6 (paperback)
  1. Lampropeltis—Juvenile literature. I. Title. II. Series.
  QL666.O636M646 2011
  597.96'2—dc22   2010041668

Editorial Credits
Brenda Haugen, editor; Ted Williams, designer; Eric Manske, production specialist

Photo Credits
Alamy: blickwinkel/Koenig, 1, David Osborn, 20, First Light/Thomas Kitchin &
Victoria Hurst, 28, imagebroker/Michael Weber, 11, John Cancalosi, 18, Papilio/
Robert Pickett, 5, Robert Clay, 23; Corbis: David A. Northcott, 16, Michael
& Patricia Fogden, 15; Dreamstime: Arpeggioangel, 24-25; Getty Images Inc.:
Visuals Unlimited/Gerold & Cynthia Merker, cover, 7, 9, 26-27; Newscom: Scott
Camazine, 12; Shutterstock: Rusty Dodson, 10

Artistic Effects
Shutterstock: Marilyn Volan

TABLE OF CONTENTS

Chapter 1

A SNAKE OF MANY COLORS

You are hiking through the forest and hear a rustling sound to your left. Stepping off the trail, you see motion. Something is rolling around in the dead leaves. It looks like two garden hoses are wrestling. Snakes! You jump back but continue to watch. One snake is black with white rings on its back. It is eating the other! It must be a kingsnake.

The King of Snakes

Kingsnakes eat other snakes. They can even eat **venomous** snakes. Snakes are not the only food in their diet, but that is what they are famous for.

Like all snakes, kingsnakes are **reptiles**. They have scales and do not produce their own heat. Scientists know kingsnakes by the genus name *Lampropeltis*. This group includes many kinds of kingsnakes as well as milksnakes. All these snakes are nonvenomous.

What's in a Name?

An old legend said snakes could drink cow's milk. Some farmers found snakes in their barns at the same time their cows stopped producing milk. They blamed the snakes. From then on, the snakes were called milksnakes. Of course, the snakes were innocent. It is impossible for snakes to suck milk from cows.

venomous—able to produce a toxic substance

reptile—a cold-blooded animal that breathes air and has a backbone; most reptiles lay eggs and have scaly skin

North
America

Europe

Asia

Africa

South
America

Australia

N
W ⬥ E
S

Antarctica

A Wide Range and Variety

Kingsnakes live in North and South America. Anywhere from the northeastern United States to California, you can find a kingsnake. The milksnake is one of the most widely found of all snakes. It can live from Canada all the way south to Ecuador.

Kingsnakes vary in size. The scarlet kingsnake only grows to be 20 inches (51 centimeters) long. Others, like the common kingsnake, can be 6 feet (1.8 meters) long. That's about as long as a bed!

The average height of an American male is 5 feet 10 inches (178 centimeters)

Kingsnakes can have many colors and patterns. Some are black or brown. Other kingsnakes are red, gray, or lavender. On top of their base color, they may have stripes, saddle-shaped bands, spots, or chainlike patterns of another color.

Kingsnake fossils have been found in the central United States. These fossils are more than 5 million years old.

Chapter 2

MEET THE ROYAL FAMILY

When a kingsnake is seen, it can be tough to figure out what kind it is. To identify the snake, it is important to understand how kingsnakes are grouped.

Within the genus *Lampropeltis*, there are eight different **species** of kingsnakes. Snakes in the same species are closely related and breed with one another.

Within those eight species, there are more than 25 **subspecies**. Snakes in the same subspecies could breed with one another, but they generally don't. Usually the distance between these snakes keeps them from breeding. For example, some may live on an island or across the country from each other.

For most animals, members of a species look alike. But kingsnakes in one species don't look alike. The gray-banded kingsnake can be white with black rings. It can also be gray with sprinkles of black. Or it can be bright orange with hourglass-shaped gray bands.

species—a specific type of animal or plant
subspecies—animals that are within the same species but
do not generally interbreed with one another

Home Sweet Home

Within their wide range, kingsnakes live in a variety of **habitats**. They may live in sandy islands, overgrown pastures, or rocky mountains. Most types of kingsnakes prefer one kind of habitat. The Louisiana milksnake likes sandy, wet forests. The gray-banded kingsnake prefers the tops of steep, rocky hills.

Kingsnakes are secretive and feel safer underground. They hide in burrows, in the cracks of rocks, or anywhere they can get out of sight.

Climate Control

Wherever they live, kingsnakes need to stay warm. But they can't make their own heat. Instead, kingsnakes depend on the heat of their surroundings to keep them comfortable. Staying underground, where the temperatures remain constant, helps them to do this.

In cooler climates kingsnakes hibernate when the temperature drops in the winter months. They find a den and sleep in it during the cold winter. As the temperatures rise in the spring, kingsnakes become active again.

Mating

One of the first things a kingsnake does in the spring is mate. As females move along the ground, they leave behind a scent like a perfume. Males follow the scent to find the females.

Hang On!

Like most snakes, New Mexico milksnakes lay wet eggs. The eggs stick together in a big lump so they do not roll around. The baby snakes are attached to the upper portions of the shells. Fluid fills the bottoms of the shells. If an egg rolls, a baby snake could drown in its shell.

Sometimes two males wrestle each other for a female. They slide up beside one another and throw their bodies into the air. The higher snake tries to push the other one toward the ground. Their tails wrap together. The fronts of their bodies push against each other. They struggle to see who will end up on top. Eventually one snake gives up and lies still on the ground.

The females lay between five and 24 leathery eggs. The nest is usually in a dead log, leaf pile, or hole. The pencil-sized babies hatch and head out to make their way in the world. They must defend themselves, keep warm, and find food all by themselves.

How fast a young kingsnake grows depends on how much food it eats. If the weather is warm and hunting is good, a young kingsnake can grow quickly. At one year, a prairie kingsnake may be twice its original size.

As it grows, a kingsnake must shed its skin. It rubs its face against a log or rock to split the skin. Then it wriggles out of the almost clear tube of skin. Looking clean and colorful, it slithers off.

Chapter 3

ON THE PROWL

Although kingsnakes eat other snakes, they have other **prey** as well. They dine on rabbits, mice, lizards, birds, eggs, and even small turtles. Some kingsnakes, such as the common kingsnake, hunt during the day. Others, such as the gray-banded kingsnake, are **nocturnal**.

Snakes, however, are ideal prey. Swallowing a wide animal, such as a turtle, puts a bulge in a kingsnake's belly. On the other hand, another snake is long and thin and slides right down the kingsnake's throat. Plus, snakes are easy for kingsnakes to hunt. Their scents linger in the grass after they pass, making it easy for a kingsnake to track them. When snakes crawl into small holes or cracks, kingsnakes can follow them right in.

prey—an animal hunted by another animal for food

nocturnal—an animal that is active at night and rests during the day

Going for the Kill

When a kingsnake crawls out of its den to go hunting, it puts its tongue to work. It flicks its tongue in and out to smell in every nook and cranny. The tongue picks up particles floating in the air. Then the snake moves its tongue to the roof of its mouth. There a pit called the Jacobson's organ senses the particles and the snake can identify the scent.

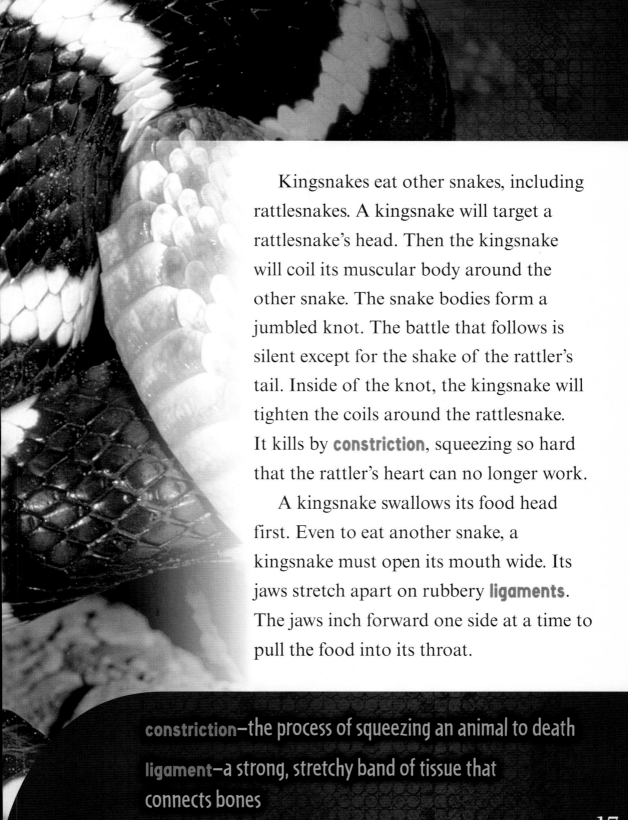

Kingsnakes eat other snakes, including rattlesnakes. A kingsnake will target a rattlesnake's head. Then the kingsnake will coil its muscular body around the other snake. The snake bodies form a jumbled knot. The battle that follows is silent except for the shake of the rattler's tail. Inside of the knot, the kingsnake will tighten the coils around the rattlesnake. It kills by **constriction**, squeezing so hard that the rattler's heart can no longer work.

A kingsnake swallows its food head first. Even to eat another snake, a kingsnake must open its mouth wide. Its jaws stretch apart on rubbery **ligaments**. The jaws inch forward one side at a time to pull the food into its throat.

constriction—the process of squeezing an animal to death

ligament—a strong, stretchy band of tissue that connects bones

Scientists don't know if kingsnakes are immune to all snake venoms, like that of the coral snake.

Venom?
No Problem!

How do kingsnakes dare hunt venomous rattlesnakes? Pit vipers, such as rattlesnakes, have pits on the sides of their heads to detect warm prey. Their venom attacks the blood and cells of their prey. It breaks apart the cells so they can't function. The venom causes a great deal of bleeding, eventually killing the animal. But kingsnakes have chemicals in their bodies that keep the pit viper venom from working.

Pit vipers are not helpless against kingsnakes. From the time they are born, they can identify the oily smell of kingsnakes and try to avoid them. If they are attacked, the vipers don't use their venom on kingsnakes. Instead, they fight back in other ways.

A pit viper sometimes raises a section of its body in the air and whacks a kingsnake with it. If that doesn't work, a viper may hide its head so a kingsnake can't grab it. A pit viper can also swell its body to look too big to eat. If all else fails, pit vipers aren't too proud to slither away.

Copycats

In nature red, yellow, and black are warning colors. They often indicate that a snake or other animal is dangerous. However, the scarlet kingsnake has these colors, and it is not venomous. This kingsnake may have changed over time to have the same colors as the deadly coral snake. That way the scarlet kingsnakes' enemies would leave it alone too.

Don't be fooled by these copycats. You can tell scarlet kingsnakes and coral snakes apart by remembering the rhyme: "Red on black, friend of Jack. Red on yellow, kill a fellow." The harmless scarlet kingsnakes have broad red bands bordered by black. Their red band never touches their yellow band. The dangerous coral snake has red bands bordered by yellow.

The Hunter Becomes the Hunted

Because of their ability to kill other snakes, the *Lampropeltis* have been given the name kingsnake. However, even a king's life is not worry-free. Kingsnake eggs and young are easy food for a variety of animals. Something as small as fire ants can threaten young kingsnakes by swarming over and biting them.

Adult kingsnakes are on the menu of skunks, coyotes, opossums, cats, and birds such as hawks and owls. Other types of snakes hunt them too. Kingsnakes even eat each other!

Chapter 4

KINGSNAKES AND YOU

Unless you spend a lot of time digging in the dirt, your chances of seeing a wild kingsnake are slim. But that doesn't mean you can't enjoy these colorful snakes. Kingsnakes make excellent pets.

A Pet King

Kingsnakes are among the most popular types of snakes kept as pets. They are gentle and easy to care for. As long as your fingers don't smell like another snake, a pet kingsnake will rarely bite. Most are small enough to be kept in a 4-foot (1.2-m) long cage. Plus they don't get sick often.

Although some pet snakes are picky eaters, kingsnakes aren't. Kingsnakes eat dead mice, which are easy for owners to provide to them.

California kingsnakes are particularly popular as pets. Small and hardy, they survive well in captivity. They also come in a rainbow of colors.

For a long time, people have been breeding kingsnakes for colors and patterns that are rare in nature. A banana yellow California kingsnake might not survive long in the wild, but it sells well at pet stores.

captivity—the condition of being kept in a cage

Some Work Required

Keeping a kingsnake as a pet does mean some work. They need a clean habitat and regular care. If the floor of its tank is damp or dirty, the snake can develop a serious blister disease. Kingsnakes need fresh water every day and food once or twice a week.

Kingsnakes are known to be escape artists. They need secure cages for their homes. A glass tank with a latching top works well. The floor should be covered with something easy to clean, such as paper, wood shavings, or indoor-outdoor carpeting.

Since they like to remain hidden, kingsnakes should have several overturned flower pots, curved pieces of bark, or rocks to hide under. Kingsnakes also need to be kept warm. They survive best at temperatures between 76 and 86 degrees Fahrenheit (24 and 30 degrees Celsius). With good care, a pet kingsnake can live more than 20 years.

Kings of the Wild

Kingsnakes that live in the wild are just that—wild. If approached, a kingsnake may rattle its tail to sound like a rattlesnake. If picked up, it might bite. It also might smear poop on anyone who tries to grab it. You should always watch a wild kingsnake from a safe distance and leave it alone.

Some wild kingsnake populations are in good shape. Other species are not doing so well. Because some species are highly prized as pets, they are still collected from the wild. In one case, a scientist watched collectors gathering Florida kingsnakes. That day they gathered every single one that they found! By eating snakes, mice, and other small animals, kingsnakes have an important job in nature. When the collectors removed the snakes from the area, they upset the balance of nature. Today there are so many captive kingsnakes to choose from that none should be taken from the wild.

In areas that have been paved or where all of the trees have been cut, kingsnakes can't find leaves to hide under. The prairie kingsnake does not like to cross roads. In heavily developed areas, these snakes have trouble finding mates. Then they can't lay eggs, and no new kingsnakes are born. When the population of the species gets too low, it is even harder for them to find mates.

With fewer kingsnakes, the animals that the snakes usually eat can survive and reproduce. Sometimes they reproduce so much that their numbers become too great. Then these animals run out of food and die too.

Respecting Kingsnakes

Some people work to help kingsnakes. The speckled kingsnake was at risk of dying out in Iowa. After people created more natural areas, the snake became more common.

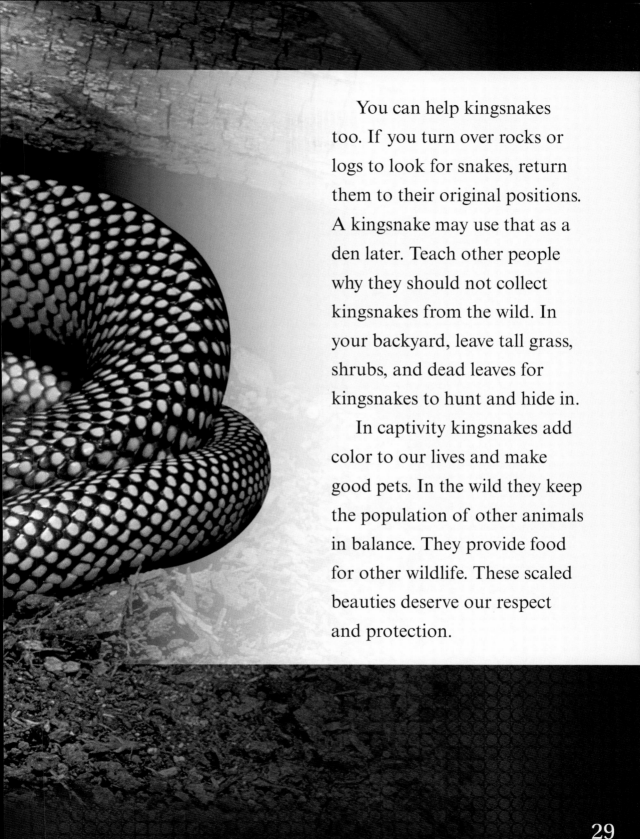

You can help kingsnakes too. If you turn over rocks or logs to look for snakes, return them to their original positions. A kingsnake may use that as a den later. Teach other people why they should not collect kingsnakes from the wild. In your backyard, leave tall grass, shrubs, and dead leaves for kingsnakes to hunt and hide in.

In captivity kingsnakes add color to our lives and make good pets. In the wild they keep the population of other animals in balance. They provide food for other wildlife. These scaled beauties deserve our respect and protection.

GLOSSARY

captivity (kap-TIV-i-tee)—the condition of being kept in a cage

constriction (con-STRIK-shun)—the process of squeezing an animal to death

habitat (HAB-uh-tat)—the natural place and conditions in which a plant or animal lives

hibernate (HI-bur-nate)—to spend a period of time in a resting state as if in a deep sleep

ligament (LIG-a-mint)—a strong, stretchy band of tissue that connects bones

nocturnal (nock-TURN-ul)—an animal that is active at night and rests during the day

prey (PRAY)—an animal hunted by another animal for food

reptile (REP-tile)—a cold-blooded animal that breathes air and has a backbone; most reptiles lay eggs and have scaly skin

species (SPEE-seez)—a specific type of animal or plant

subspecies (sub-SPEE-seez)—animals that are within the same species but do not generally interbreed with one another

venomous (VEN-uhm-us)—able to produce a toxic substance

READ MORE

Hoff, Mary. *Snakes.* The Wild World of Animals. Mankato, Minn.: Creative Education, 2007.

Simon, Seymour. *Poisonous Animals.* New York: Scholastic, 2007.

White, Nancy. *King Cobras: The Biggest Venomous Snakes of All!* Fangs. New York: Bearport Publishing, 2009.

INTERNET SITES

FactHound offers a safe, fun way to find Internet sites related to this book. All of the sites on FactHound have been researched by our staff.

Here's all you do:

Visit *www.facthound.com*

Type in this code: 9781429660136

INDEX